WISE QUOTES: SHAKESPEARE

(401 SHAKESPEARE QUOTES)

Vol. 1

Rowan Stevens

A coward dies a thousand times before his death, but the valiant taste of death but once. It seems to me most strange that men should fear, seeing that death, a necessary end, will come when it will come.

A glooming peace this morning with it brings;
The sun, for sorrow, will not show his head:
Go hence, to have more talk of these sad things;
Some shall be pardon'd, and some punished:
For never was a story of more woe
Than this of Juliet and her Romeo.

A little more than kin, a little less than kind.

A miracle. Here's our own hands against our hearts. Come, I will have thee, but by this light I take thee for pity.

A rose by any other name would smell as sweet.

A sad tale's best for winter: I have one of sprites and goblins.

A wretched soul, bruised with adversity,
We bid be quiet when we hear it cry;
But were we burdened with light weight of pain,
As much or more we should ourselves complain.

A young woman in love always looks like patience on a monument smiling at grief.

Alas, poor Yorick! I knew him, Horatio: a fellow of infinite jest, of most excellent fancy: he hath borne me on his back a thousand times; and now, how abhorred in my imagination it is! my gorge rims at it. Here hung those lips that I have kissed I know not how oft. Where be your gibes now? your gambols? your songs? your flashes of merriment, that were wont to set the table on a roar? Not one now, to mock your own grinning? quite chap-fallen?

Alas, that love, so gentle in his view,
Should be so tyrannous and rough in proof!

All causes shall give way: I am in blood
Stepp'd in so far that, should I wade no more,
Returning were as tedious as go o'er.

All that glisters is not gold;
Often have you heard that told:
Many a man his life has sold
But my outside to behold:
Gilded tombs do worms enfold
Had you been as wise as bold,
Your in limbs, in judgment old,
Your answer had not been in'scroll'd
Fare you well: your suit is cold.' Cold, indeed, and labour lost:
Then, farewell, heat and welcome, frost!

All the world's a stage,
And all the men and women merely players;
They have their exits and their entrances,
And one man in his time plays many parts,
His acts being seven ages. At first, the infant,
Mewling and puking in the nurse's arms.
Then the whining schoolboy, with his satchel
And shining morning face, creeping like snail

Unwillingly to school. And then the lover,
Sighing like furnace, with a woeful ballad
Made to his mistress' eyebrow. Then a soldier,
Full of strange oaths and bearded like the pard,
Jealous in honor, sudden and quick in quarrel,
Seeking the bubble reputation
Even in the cannon's mouth. And then the justice,
In fair round belly with good capon lined,
With eyes severe and beard of formal cut,
Full of wise saws and modern instances;
And so he plays his part. The sixth age shifts
Into the lean and slippered pantaloon,
With spectacles on nose and pouch on side;
His youthful hose, well saved, a world too wide
For his shrunk shank, and his big manly voice,
Turning again toward childish treble, pipes
And whistles in his sound. Last scene of all,
That ends this strange eventful history,
Is second childishness and mere oblivion,
Sans teeth, sans eyes, sans taste, sans everything.

All things are ready, if our mind be so.

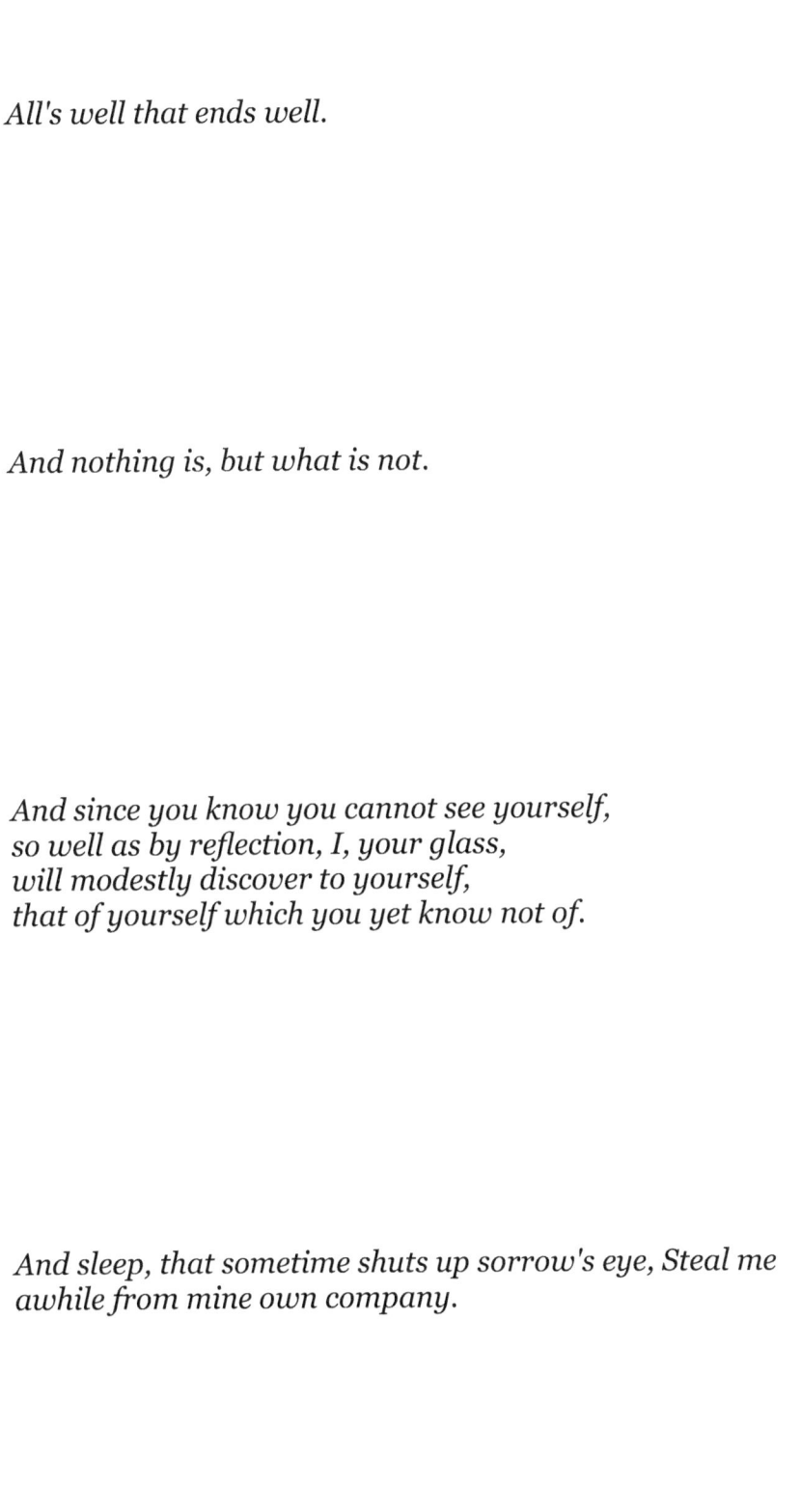

All's well that ends well.

And nothing is, but what is not.

And since you know you cannot see yourself,
so well as by reflection, I, your glass,
will modestly discover to yourself,
that of yourself which you yet know not of.

And sleep, that sometime shuts up sorrow's eye, Steal me
awhile from mine own company.

And therefore, — since I cannot prove a lover,
To entertain these fair well-spoken days, —
I am determined to prove a villain,
And hate the idle pleasures of these days.

And this our life, exempt from public haunt, finds tongues in
trees, books in the running brooks, sermons in stones, and
good in everything. I would not change it.

And thus I clothe my naked villainy
With odd old ends stol'n out of holy writ;
And seem a saint, when most I play the devil.

And worse I may be yet: the worst is not
So long as we can say 'This is the worst.

And yet, to say the truth, reason and love keep little company
together nowadays.

Angels are bright still, though the brightest fell.
Though all things foul would wear the brows of grace,
Yet Grace must still look so.

April hath put a spirit of youth in everything.

Are you sure
That we are awake?
It seems to me
That yet we sleep, we dream

As flies to wanton boys are we to the gods.
They kill us for their sport.

Awake, dear heart, awake. Thou hast slept well. Awake.

Banish'd from those we love is self from self: a deadly
banishment!

Be great in act, as you have been in thought.

Be not afeard; the isle is full of noises,
Sounds, and sweet airs, that give delight and hurt not.
Sometimes a thousand twangling instruments
Will hum about mine ears; and sometime voices,
That, if I then had waked after long sleep,
Will make me sleep again: and then, in dreaming,
The clouds methought would open, and show riches
Ready to drop upon me; that, when I waked,
I cried to dream again.

Be not afraid of greatness. Some are born great, some
achieve greatness, and others have greatness thrust upon
them.

BENEDICK
Fair Beatrice, I thank you for your pains.

BEATRICE
I took no more pains for those thanks than you take pains to thank me: if it had been painful, I would not have come.

BENVOLIO
What sadness lengthens Romeo's hours?

ROMEO
Not having that, which, having, makes them short.

Better a witty fool, than a foolish wit.

Better three hours too soon than a minute too late.

Beware the ides of March.

Bid me run, and I will strive with things impossible.

Blood will have blood.

Blow, winds, and crack your cheeks! Rage! Blow!
You cataracts and hurricanoes, spout
Till you have drenched our teeples, drowned the cocks!
You sulphurour and thought-executing fires,
Vaunt-couriers to oak-cleaving thunderbolts,
Singe my white head! And thou, all-shaking thunder,
Strike flat the thick rotundity o' the world!
Crack nature's molds, all germens spill at once
That make ingrateful man!

Brevity is the soul of wit.

But break, my heart, for I must hold my tongue.

But I am constant as the Northern Star,
Of whose true fixed and resting quality
There is no fellow in the firmament.

But I will wear my heart upon my sleeve
For daws to peck at: I am not what I am.

But man, proud man,
Dress'd in a little brief authority,
Most ignorant of what he's most assur'd—
His glassy essence—like an angry ape
Plays such fantastic tricks before high heaven
As makes the angels weep; who, with our spleens,
Would all themselves laugh mortal.

But, soft! what light through yonder window breaks?
It is the east, and Juliet is the sun.
Arise, fair sun, and kill the envious moon,
Who is already sick and pale with grief,
That thou, her maid, art far more fair than she.
Be not her maid, since she is envious;
Her vestal livery is but sick and green
And none but fools do wear it; cast it off.
It is my lady, O, it is my love!
Oh, that she knew she were!

By the pricking of my thumbs,
Something wicked this way comes.

Come what come may, time and the hour run through the
roughest day.

Come, gentle night; come, loving, black-browed night;
Give me my Romeo; and, when I shall die,
Take him and cut him out in little stars,
And he will make the face of heaven so fine
That all the world will be in love with night...

Come, you spirits
That tend on mortal thoughts! Unsex me here,
And fill me from the crown to the toe top full
Of direst cruelty; make thick my blood,
Stop up the access and passage to remorse,
That no compunctious visitings of nature
Shake my fell purpose, nor keep peace between
The effect and it! Come to my woman's breasts,
And take my milk for gall, you murdering ministers,
Wherever in your sightless substances
You wait on nature's mischief! Come, thick night,
And pall thee in the dunnest smoke of hell,
That my keen knife see not the wound it makes,
Nor Heaven peep through the blanket of the dark,
To cry Hold, hold!

Confusion now hath made his masterpiece.

Conscience doth make cowards of us all.

Cowards die many times before their deaths;
The valiant never taste of death but once.
Of all the wonders that I yet have heard,
It seems to me most strange that men should fear;
Seeing that death, a necessary end,
Will come when it will come.

Cry havoc and let slip the dogs of war!

Death, a necessary end, will come when it will come.

Death, that hath suck'd the honey of thy breath hath had no power yet upon thy beauty.

DEMETRIUS
Villain, what hast thou done?

AARON
That which thou canst not undo.

CHIRON
Thou hast undone our mother.

AARON
Villain, I have done thy mother.

Did my heart love till now? forswear it, sight! For I ne'er saw true beauty till this night.

Discretion is the better part of valor.

Dispute not with her: she is lunatic.

Do not swear by the moon, for she changes constantly. Then your love would also change.

Do you bite your thumb at us, sir?

Do you not know I am a woman? when I think, I must speak.

Don't waste your love on somebody, who doesn't value it.

Double, double, toil and trouble;
Fire burn, and cauldron bubble!

Doubt thou the stars are fire;
Doubt that the sun doth move;
Doubt truth to be a liar;
But never doubt I love.

Educated men are so impressive!

Et tu, Brute?

Excellent wretch! Perdition catch my soul But I do love thee!
and when I love thee not, Chaos is come again.

Exit, pursued by a bear.

Expectation is the root of all heartache.

Eye of newt, and toe of frog,
Wool of bat, and tongue of dog,
Adder's fork, and blind-worm's sting,
Lizard's leg, and owlet's wing,—
For a charm of powerful trouble,
Like a hell-broth boil and bubble.
Double, double toil and trouble;
Fire burn, and caldron bubble.

Eyes, look your last!
Arms, take your last embrace!

And, lips, oh you the doors of breath, seal with a righteous
kiss a dateless bargain to engrossing death!

Fair is foul, and foul is fair, hover through fog and filthy air.

False face must hide what the false heart doth know.

Fear no more the heat o' the sun,
Nor the furious winter's rages;
Thou thy worldly task hast done,
Home art gone, and ta'en thy wages;
Golden lads and girls all must,
As chimney-sweepers, come to dust.

Fear no more the frown o' the great;

Thou art past the tyrant's stroke:
Care no more to clothe and eat;
To thee the reed is as the oak:
The sceptre, learning, physic, must
All follow this, and come to dust.

Fear no more the lightning-flash,
Nor the all-dreaded thunder-stone;
Fear not slander, censure rash;
Thou hast finished joy and moan;
All lovers young, all lovers must
Consign to thee, and come to dust.

No exorciser harm thee!
Nor no witchcraft charm thee!
Ghost unlaid forbear thee!
Nothing ill come near thee!
Quiet consummation have;
And renownéd be thy grave!

For God's sake, let us sit upon the ground
And tell sad stories of the death of kings;
How some have been deposed; some slain in war,
Some haunted by the ghosts they have deposed;
Some poison'd by their wives: some sleeping kill'd;
All murder'd: for within the hollow crown
That rounds the mortal temples of a king
Keeps Death his court and there the antic sits,
Scoffing his state and grinning at his pomp,
Allowing him a breath, a little scene,
To monarchize, be fear'd and kill with looks,

Infusing him with self and vain conceit,
As if this flesh which walls about our life,
Were brass impregnable, and humour'd thus
Comes at the last and with a little pin
Bores through his castle wall, and farewell king!

For I have sworn thee fair, and thought thee bright,
Who art as black as hell, as dark as night.

For it falls out
That what we have we prize not to the worth
Whiles we enjoy it, but being lacked and lost,
Why, then we rack the value, then we find
The virtue that possession would not show us
While it was ours.

For man is a giddy thing, and this is my conclusion.

For never was a story of more woe than this of Juliet and her Romeo.

For she had eyes and chose me.

For sweetest things turn sourest by their deeds; Lillies that fester smell far worse than weeds.

For which of my bad parts didst thou first fall in love with me?

For you, in my respect, are all the world.
Then how can it be said I am alone
When all the world is here to look on me?

Friends, Romans, countrymen, lend me your ears;
I come to bury Caesar, not to praise him;
The evil that men do lives after them,
The good is oft interred with their bones,
So let it be with Caesar ... The noble Brutus
Hath told you Caesar was ambitious:
If it were so, it was a grievous fault,
And grievously hath Caesar answered it ...
Here, under leave of Brutus and the rest,
(For Brutus is an honourable man;
So are they all; all honourable men)
Come I to speak in Caesar's funeral ...
He was my friend, faithful and just to me:
But Brutus says he was ambitious;
And Brutus is an honourable man....
He hath brought many captives home to Rome,
Whose ransoms did the general coffers fill:

Did this in Caesar seem ambitious?
When that the poor have cried, Caesar hath wept:
Ambition should be made of sterner stuff:
Yet Brutus says he was ambitious;
And Brutus is an honourable man.
You all did see that on the Lupercal
I thrice presented him a kingly crown,
Which he did thrice refuse: was this ambition?
Yet Brutus says he was ambitious;
And, sure, he is an honourable man.
I speak not to disprove what Brutus spoke,
But here I am to speak what I do know.
You all did love him once, not without cause:
What cause withholds you then to mourn for him?
O judgement! thou art fled to brutish beasts,
And men have lost their reason.... Bear with me;
My heart is in the coffin there with Caesar,
And I must pause till it come back to me

From this day to the ending of the world,
But we in it shall be remembered-
We few, we happy few, we band of brothers;
For he to-day that sheds his blood with me
Shall be my brother; be he ne'er so vile,
This day shall gentle his condition;
And gentlemen in England now-a-bed
Shall think themselves accurs'd they were not here,
And hold their manhoods cheap whiles any speaks
That fought with us upon Saint Crispin's day.

From women's eyes this doctrine I derive:
They sparkle still the right Promethean fire;
They are the books, the arts, the academes,
That show, contain and nourish all the world.

Full fathom five thy father lies;
Of his bones are coral made;
Those are pearls that were his eyes:
Nothing of him that doth fade,
But doth suffer a sea-change
Into something rich and strange.
Sea-nymphs hourly ring his knell: Ding-dong
Hark! now I hear them,—Ding-dong, bell.

Get thee to a nunnery.

Give every man thine ear, but few thy voice; Take each man's censure, but reserve thy judgment.

Give me my robe, put on my crown; I have Immortal longings in me

Give me my sin again.

Give me that man that is not passion's slave, and I will wear him in my heart's core, in my heart of heart, as I do thee.

Give sorrow words; the grief that does not speak knits up the o-er wrought heart and bids it break.

Go to your bosom; Knock there, and ask your heart what it doth know.

Go wisely and slowly. Those who rush stumble and fall.

God hath given you one face, and you make yourself another.

Good name in man and woman, dear my lord,
Is the immediate jewel of their souls:
Who steals my purse steals trash; 'tis something, nothing;
'twas mine, 'tis his, and has been slave to thousands;
But he that filches from me my good name
Robs me of that which not enriches him,
And makes me poor indeed.

Good night, good night! parting is such sweet sorrow,
That I shall say good night till it be morrow.

Good wombs have borne bad sons.

Have more than you show,
Speak less than you know.

He jests at scars that never felt a wound.

He that hath a beard is more than a youth, and he that hath
no beard is less than a man. He that is more than a youth is
not for me, and he that is less than a man, I am not for him.

He that is thy friend indeed,
He will help thee in thy need:
If thou sorrow, he will weep;
If thou wake, he cannot sleep:
Thus of every grief in heart
He with thee doth bear a part.

These are certain signs to know
Faithful friend from flattering foe.

He's of the colour of the nutmeg. And of the heat of the ginger.... he is pure air and fire; and the dull elements of earth and water never appear in him, but only in patient stillness while his rider mounts him; he is indeed a horse, and all other jades you may call beasts.

Hell is empty and all the devils are here.

His life was gentle; and the elements
So mixed in him, that Nature might stand up
And say to all the world, THIS WAS A MAN!

How art thou out of breath when thou hast breath
To say to me that thou art out of breath?

How far that little candle throws his beams! So shines a good
deed in a weary world.

How poor are they that have not patience! What wound did
ever heal but by degrees?

How sharper than a serpent's tooth it is To have a thankless
child!

I am a Jew. Hath not a Jew eyes? Hath not a Jew hands, organs, dimensions, senses, affections, passions; fed with the same food, hurt with the same weapons, subject to the same diseases, heal'd by the same means, warm'd and cool'd by the same winter and summer, as a Christian is?

If you prick us, do we not bleed? If you tickle us, do we not laugh? If you poison us, do we not die?

And if you wrong us, do we not revenge? If we are like you in the rest, we will resemble you in that.

I am a man more sinned against than sinning.

I am but mad north-north-west. When the wind is southerly, I know a hawk from a handsaw.

I am not bound to please thee with my answers.

I am very proud, revengeful, ambitious, with more offences at my beck than I have thoughts to put them in, imagination to give them shape, or time to act them in.

I can see he's not in your good books,' said the messenger. 'No, and if he were I would burn my library.

I could be bounded in a nutshell and count myself king of infinite space.

I dare do all that may become a man;
Who dares do more, is none.

I defy you, stars.

I do feel it gone,
But know not how it went.

I do love nothing in the world so well as you- is not that
strange?

I had rather hear my dog bark at a crow, than a man swear he loves me.

I have had a most rare vision. I have had a dream, past the wit of man to say what dream it was.

I have no spur
To prick the sides of my intent, but only
Vaulting ambition, which o'erleaps itself
And falls on the other.

I hold the world but as the world, Gratiano,
A stage where every man must play a part,
And mine a sad one.

I kissed thee ere I killed thee. No way but this,
Killing myself, to die upon a kiss.

I know a bank where the wild thyme blows,
Where oxlips and the nodding violet grows,
Quite over-canopied with luscious woodbine,
With sweet musk-roses and with eglantine.

I like this place and could willingly waste my time in it.

I love you with so much of my heart that none is left to protest.

I loved Ophelia. Forty thousand brothers could not, with all their quantity of love, make up my sum.

I must be cruel only to be kind;
Thus bad begins, and worse remains behind.

I must be gone and live, or stay and die.

I pray you, do not fall in love with me, for I am falser than vows made in wine.

I say there is no darkness but ignorance.

I wasted time, and now doth time waste me;
For now hath time made me his numbering clock:
My thoughts are minutes; and with sighs they jar
Their watches on unto mine eyes, the outward watch,
Whereto my finger, like a dial's point,
Is pointing still, in cleansing them from tears.
Now sir, the sound that tells what hour it is
Are clamorous groans, which strike upon my heart,
Which is the bell: so sighs and tears and groans
Show minutes, times, and hours.

I will live in thy heart, die in thy lap, and be buried in thy
eyes—and moreover, I will go with thee to thy uncle's.

I wish my horse had the speed of your tongue.

I would not put a thief in my mouth to steal my brains.

I would not wish any companion in the world but you.

I'll follow thee and make a heaven of hell,
To die upon the hand I love so well.

If I be waspish, best beware my sting.

If love be rough with you, be rough with love. Prick love for pricking and you beat love down.

If music be the food of love, play on,
Give me excess of it; that surfeiting,
The appetite may sicken, and so die.

If there is a good will, there is great way.

If we are true to ourselves, we cannot be false to anyone.

If we shadows have offended,
Think but this, and all is mended,
That you have but slumbered here
While these visions did appear.
And this weak and idle theme,
No more yielding but a dream,
Gentles, do not reprehend:
If you pardon, we will mend:
And, as I am an honest Puck,
If we have unearned luck
Now to 'scape the serpent's tongue,
We will make amends ere long;
Else the Puck a liar call;
So, good night unto you all.
Give me your hands, if we be friends,
And Robin shall restore amends.

Ill met by moonlight, proud Titania.

In black ink my love may still shine bright.

In jest, there is truth.

In nature there's no blemish but the mind.
None can be called deformed but the unkind.

In time we hate that which we often fear.

Is it not strange that sheep's guts could hail souls out of men's bodies?

Is love a tender thing? It is too rough, too rude, too boisterous, and it pricks like thorn.

It is not in the stars to hold our destiny but in ourselves.

It is silliness to live when to live is torment, and then have we a prescription to die when death is our physician.

It provokes the desire, but it takes away the performance

It's easy for someone to joke about scars if they've never been cut.

JAQUES
Rosalind is your love's name?

ORLANDO
Yes, just.

JAQUES
I do not like her name.

ORLANDO
There was no thought of pleasing you when she was christened.

Journeys end in lovers meeting.

LEONATO
Well, niece, I hope to see you one day fitted with a husband.

BEATRICE
Not till God make men of some other metal than earth. Would it not grieve a woman to be overmastered with a pierce of valiant dust? to make an account of her life to a clod of wayward marl? No, uncle, I'll none: Adam's sons are my brethren; and, truly, I hold it a sin to match in my kindred.

Let me be that I am and seek not to alter me.

Let me not to the marriage of true minds
Admit impediments. Love is not love
Which alters when it alteration finds,
Or bends with the remover to remove.
O no, it is an ever-fixed mark
That looks on tempests and is never shaken;
It is the star to every wand'ring barque,
Whose worth's unknown, although his height be taken.
Love's not Time's fool, though rosy lips and cheeks
Within his bending sickle's compass come;
Love alters not with his brief hours and weeks,
But bears it out even to the edge of doom.
If this be error and upon me proved,
I never writ, nor no man ever loved.

Let us not burthen our remembrance with
A heaviness that's gone.

Let's talk of graves, of worms, and epitaphs;
Make dust our paper and with rainy eyes
Write sorrow on the bosom of the earth,
Let's choose executors and talk of wills

Life is a tale
Told by an idiot, full of sound and fury,
Signifying nothing.

Life... is a paradise to what we fear of death.

Life's but a walking shadow, a poor player,
That struts and frets his hour upon the stage,
And then is heard no more. It is a tale
Told by an idiot, full of sound and fury,
Signifying nothing.

Like madness is the glory of this life.

Listen to many, speak to a few.

Look like the innocent flower,
But be the serpent under it.

Lord, what fools these mortals be!

Love all, trust a few,
Do wrong to none: be able for thine enemy
Rather in power than use; and keep thy friend
Under thy own life's key: be check'd for silence,
But never tax'd for speech.

Love comforteth like sunshine after rain.

Love goes toward love as schoolboys from their books,
But love from love, toward school with heavy looks.

Love is a smoke made with the fume of sighs;
Being purg'd, a fire sparkling in lovers' eyes;
Being vex'd, a sea nourish'd with lovers' tears;
What is it else? A madness most discreet,
A choking gall, and a preserving sweet.

Here's what love is: a smoke made out of lovers' sighs. When the smoke clears, love is a fire burning in your lover's eyes. If you frustrate love, you get an ocean made out of lovers' tears. What else is love? It's a wise form of madness. It's a sweet lozenge that you choke on.

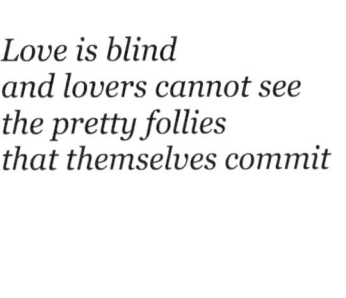

Love is blind
and lovers cannot see
the pretty follies
that themselves commit

Love is heavy and light, bright and dark, hot and cold, sick
and healthy, asleep and awake- its everything except what it
is!

Love is merely a madness; and, I tell you, deserves as well a
dark house and a whip as madmen do; and the reason why
they are not so punish'd and cured is that the lunacy is so
ordinary that the whippers are in love too.

Love is not love
Which alters when it alteration finds,
Or bends with the remover to remove.
O no, it is an ever-fixed mark
That looks on tempests and is never shaken;
It is the star to every wand'ring bark,
Whose worth's unknown, although his height be taken.

Love looks not with the eyes, but with the mind,
And therefore is winged Cupid painted blind.

Love me!... Why?

Love moderately. Long love doth so.
Too swift arrives as tardy as too slow.

Love each other in moderation. That is the key to long-lasting love. Too fast is as bad as too slow.

Love sought is good, but giv'n unsought is better.

Love's stories written in love's richest books.
To fan the moonbeams from his sleeping eyes..

Lovers and madmen have such seething brains,
Such shaping fantasies, that apprehend
More than cool reason ever comprehends.
The lunatic, the lover and the poet
Are of imagination all compact:
One sees more devils than vast hell can hold,
That is, the madman: the lover, all as frantic,

Sees Helen's beauty in a brow of Egypt:
The poet's eye, in fine frenzy rolling,
Doth glance from heaven to earth, from earth to heaven;
And as imagination bodies forth
The forms of things unknown, the poet's pen
Turns them to shapes and gives to airy nothing
A local habitation and a name.

Cure her of that! Canst thou not minister to a mind diseased,
pluck from the memory a rooted sorrow, raze out the written
troubles of the brain, and with some sweet oblivious antidote
cleanse the stuffed bosom of that perilous stuff which weighs
upon her heart.

Madness in great ones must not unwatched go.

Make death proud to take us.

Many a true word hath been spoken in jest.

Me, poor man, my library
Was dukedom large enough.

Men at some time are masters of their fates. The fault, dear
Brutus, is not in our stars, but in ourselves, that we are
underlings.

Men have died from time to time, and worms have eaten them, but not for love.

Men in rage strike those that wish them best.

Men of few words are the best men.

Men should be what they seem.

Men's evil manners live in brass; their virtues we write in water.

Methought I heard a voice cry, Sleep no more!
Macbeth does murder sleep, - the innocent sleep;
Sleep that knits up the ravell'd sleave of care,
The death of each day's life, sore labour's bath,
Balm of hurt minds, great nature's second course,
Chief nourisher in life's feast.

Misery acquaints a man with strange bedfellows.

More of your conversation would infect my brain.

Most friendship is feigning, most loving mere folly.

My bounty is as boundless as the sea,
My love as deep; the more I give to thee,
The more I have, for both are infinite.

My Crown is in my heart, not on my head:
Not deck'd with Diamonds, and Indian stones:
Nor to be seen: my Crown is call'd Content,
A Crown it is, that seldom Kings enjoy.

My hands are of your color, but I shame to wear a heart so
white.

My mistress' eyes are nothing like the sun;
Coral is far more red than her lips' red;
If snow be white, why then her breasts are dun;
If hairs be wires, black wires grow on her head.
I have seen roses damask'd, red and white,
But no such roses see I in her cheeks;
And in some perfumes is there more delight
Than in the breath that from my mistress reeks.
I love to hear her speak, yet well I know
That music hath a far more pleasing sound;
I grant I never saw a goddess go;
My mistress, when she walks, treads on the ground:
And yet, by heaven, I think my love as rare
As any she belied with false compare.

My only love sprung from my only hate!
Too early seen unknown, and known too late!
Prodigious birth of love it is to me,
That I must love a loathed enemy.

My soul is in the sky.

My tongue will tell the anger of my heart, or else my heart concealing it will break.

My words fly up, my thoughts remain below: Words without thoughts never to heaven go.

No legacy is so rich as honesty.

No sooner met but they looked; no sooner looked but they loved; no sooner loved but they sighed; no sooner sighed but they asked one another the reason; no sooner knew the reason but they sought the remedy; and in these degrees have they made a pair of stairs to marriage...

No, no, I am but shadow of myself:
You are deceived, my substance is not here;

No, no, no, no! Come, let's away to prison:
We two alone will sing like birds i' the cage:
When thou dost ask me blessing, I'll kneel down,
And ask of thee forgiveness: so we'll live,
And pray, and sing, and tell old tales, and laugh
At gilded butterflies, and hear poor rogues
Talk of court news; and we'll talk with them too,
Who loses and who wins; who's in, who's out;
And take upon's the mystery of things,
As if we were God's spies: and we'll wear out,
In a wall'd prison, packs and sects of great ones,
That ebb and flow by the moon.

*Not a whit, we defy augury: there's a special
providence in the fall of a sparrow. If it be now,
'tis not to come; if it be not to come, it will be
now; if it be not now, yet it will come: the
readiness is all.*

Not that I loved Caesar less, but that I loved Rome more.

Nothing will come of nothing: speak again.

*Now cracks a noble heart. Good-night, sweet prince;
And flights of angels sing thee to thy rest.*

Now I will believe that there are unicorns...

Now is the winter of our discontent
Made glorious summer by this sun of York;
And all the clouds that lour'd upon our house
In the deep bosom of the ocean buried.

O God, I could be bound in a nutshell, and count myself a king
of infinite space – were it not that I have bad dreams.

O me, you juggler, you canker-blossom, you thief of love!

O Romeo, Romeo, wherefore art thou Romeo?
Deny thy father refuse thy name, thou art thyself thou not a
montegue, what is montegue? tis nor hand nor foot nor any
other part belonging to a man
What is in a name?
That which we call a rose by any other name would smell as
sweet,
So Romeo would were he not Romeo called retain such dear
perfection to which he owes without that title,
Romeo, Doth thy name!
And for that name which is no part of thee, take all thyself.

O serpent heart hid with a flowering face!
Did ever a dragon keep so fair a cave?
Beautiful tyrant, feind angelical, dove feather raven, wolvish-
ravening lamb! Despised substance of devinest show, just
opposite to what thou justly seemest - A dammed saint, an
honourable villain!

O sleep, O gentle sleep, Nature's soft nurse, how have I
frightened thee. That thou no more will weigh my eyelids
down, And steep my senses in forgetfulness?

O teach me how I should forget to think.

O time, thou must untangle this, not I.
It is too hard a knot for me t'untie.

O, beware, my lord, of jealousy;
It is the green-ey'd monster, which doth mock
The meat it feeds on. That cuckold lives in bliss,
Who, certain of his fate, loves not his wronger:
But O, what damnèd minutes tells he o'er
Who dotes, yet doubts, suspects, yet strongly loves!

O, brave new world
that has such people in't!

O, full of scorpions is my mind!

O, here
Will I set up my everlasting rest,
And shake the yoke of inauspicious stars
From this world-wearied flesh. Eyes, look your last!
Arms, take your last embrace! and, lips, O you
The doors of breath, seal with a righteous kiss
A dateless bargain to engrossing death!

O, let me kiss that hand!

Let me wipe it first; it smells of mortality.

O, swear not by the moon, th' inconstant moon,
That monthly changes in her circle orb,
Lest that thy love prove likewise variable.

O, when she's angry, she is keen and shrewd! She was a vixen
when she went to school; And though she be but little, she is
fierce.

O, wonder!
How many goodly creatures are there here!
How beauteous mankind is! O brave new world,
That has such people in't!

O! she doth teach the torches to burn bright
It seems she hangs upon the cheek of night
Like a rich jewel in an Ethiop's ear;
Beauty too rich for use, for earth too dear.

Of all the wonders that I have heard,
It seems to me most strange that men should fear;
Seeing death, a necessary end,
Will come when it will come.

DOGBERRY
Marry, sir, they have committed false report; moreover, they
have spoken untruths; secondarily, they are slanders; sixth
and lastly, they have
belied a lady; thirdly, they have verified unjust things; and,
to conclude, they are lying knaves.

Oh why rebuke you him that loves you so?
Lay breath so bitter on your bitter foe.

Oh, I am fortune's fool!

OLIVIA
How does he love me?

VIOLA
With adoration, with fertile tears,
With groans that thunder love, with sighs of fire.

Once more unto the breach, dear friends, once more;
Or close the wall up with our English dead!
In peace there's nothing so becomes a man

As modest stillness and humility:
But when the blast of war blows in our ears,
Then imitate the action of the tiger.

One fire burns out another's burning,
One pain is lessen'd by another's anguish.

One half of me is yours, the other half is yours,
Mine own, I would say; but if mine, then yours,
And so all yours.

One may smile, and smile, and be a villain.

One pain is lessened by another's anguish. ... Take thou some new infection to thy eye, And the rank poison of the old will die.

Our doubts are traitors,
and make us lose the good we oft might win,
by fearing to attempt.

Our revels now are ended. These our actors,
As I foretold you, were all spirits and
Are melted into air, into thin air:
And, like the baseless fabric of this vision,
The cloud-capp'd towers, the gorgeous palaces,
The solemn temples, the great globe itself,
Yea, all which it inherit, shall dissolve
And, like this insubstantial pageant faded,
Leave not a rack behind. We are such stuff
As dreams are made on, and our little life
Is rounded with a sleep.

Out of her favour, where I am in love.

Out of my sight! Thou dost infect mine eyes.

Out, damned spot! out, I say!

Out, out, brief candle! Life's but a walking shadow, a poor player that struts and frets his hour upon the stage and is heard no more. It is a tale told by an idiot, full of sound and fury, signifying nothing.

Parting is such sweet sorrow that I shall say goodnight till it be morrow.

Peace? I hate the word as I hate hell and all Montagues.

Presume not that I am the thing I was.

Remember me.

Reputation is an idle and most false imposition; oft got without merit, and lost without deserving.

Romeo, Romeo, wherefore art thou Romeo?

ROMEO
If I profane with my unworthiest hand
This holy shrine, the gentle fine is this:
My lips, two blushing pilgrims, ready stand
To smooth that rough touch with a tender kiss.

JULIET
Good pilgrim, you do wrong your hand too much,
Which mannerly devotion shows in this;
For saints have hands that pilgrims' hands do touch,
And palm to palm is holy palmers' kiss.

Rude am I in my speech, And little blessed with the soft phrase of peace.

See how she leans her cheek upon her hand.
O, that I were a glove upon that hand
That I might touch that cheek!

Self-love, my liege, is not so vile a sin, as self-neglecting.

Shall I compare thee to a summer's day?
Thou art more lovely and more temperate:
Rough winds do shake the darling buds of May,
And summer's lease hath all too short a date:
Sometimes too hot the eye of heaven shines,
And too often is his gold complexion dimm'd:

And every fair from fair sometimes declines,
By chance or natures changing course untrimm'd;
By thy eternal summer shall not fade,
Nor lose possession of that fair thou owest;
Nor shall Death brag thou wander'st in his shade,
When in eternal lines to time thou growest:
So long as men can breathe or eyes can see,
So long lives this and this gives life to thee.

She lov'd me for the dangers I had pass'd,
And I lov'd her that she did pity them

She never told her love, but let concealment, like a worm 'i th'
bud, feed on her damask cheek. She pinned in thought; and,
with a green and yellow melancholy, she sat like Patience on
a monument, smiling at grief. Was not this love indeed? We
men may say more, swear more; but indeed our shows are
more than will; for we still prove much in our vows but little
in our love.

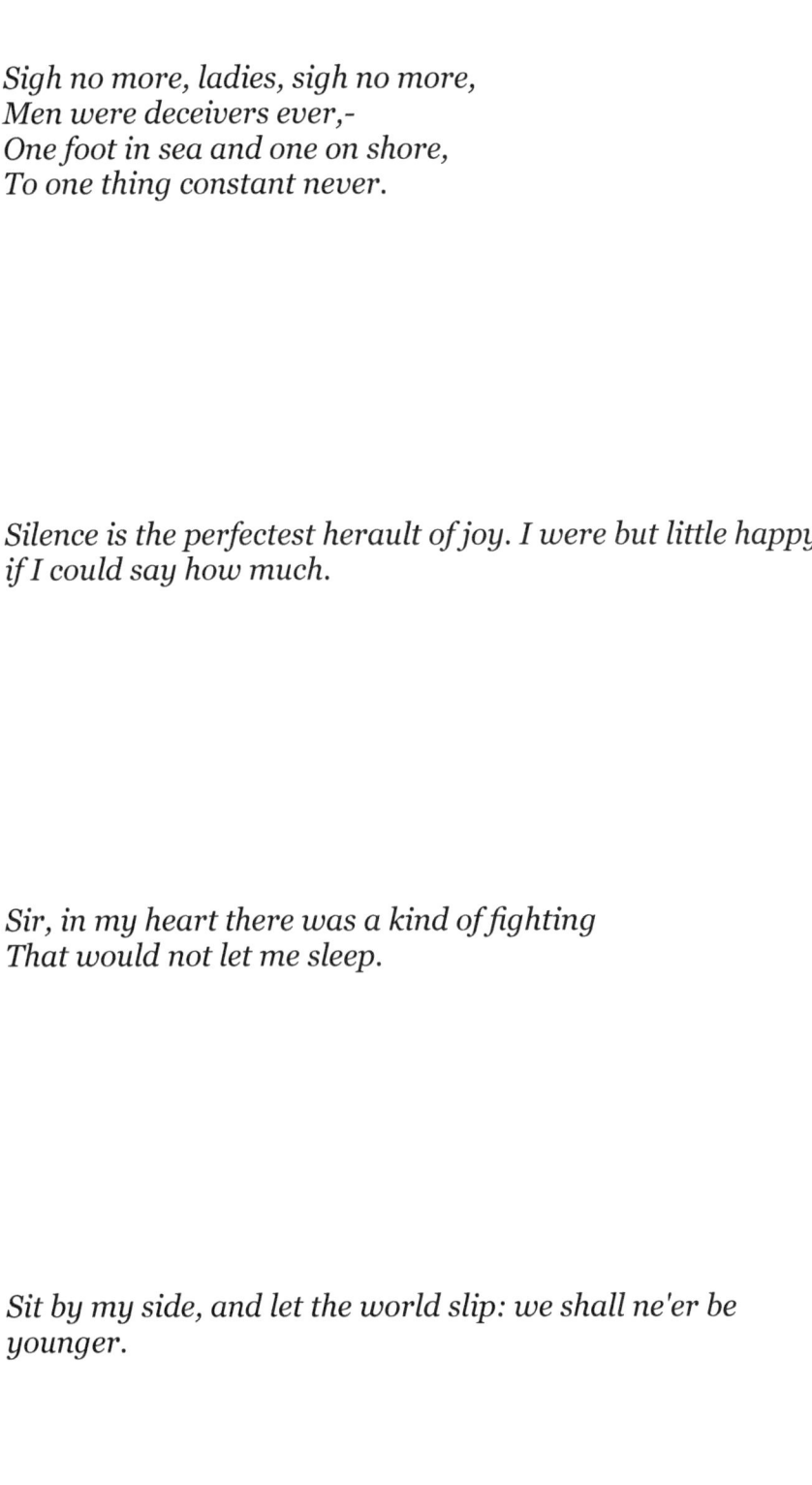

Sigh no more, ladies, sigh no more,
Men were deceivers ever,-
One foot in sea and one on shore,
To one thing constant never.

Silence is the perfectest herault of joy. I were but little happy
if I could say how much.

Sir, in my heart there was a kind of fighting
That would not let me sleep.

Sit by my side, and let the world slip: we shall ne'er be
younger.

So fair and foul a day I have not seen.

So full of artless jealousy is guilt,
It spills itself in fearing to be spilt.

So long as men can breathe, or eyes can see,
So long lives this, and this gives life to thee.

So we grew together,
Like to a double cherry, seeming parted,
But yet an union in partition,
Two lovely berries moulded on one stem.

So wise so young, they say, do never live long.

Some Cupid kills with arrows, some with traps.

Some rise by sin, and some by virtues fall.

Something is rotten in the state of Denmark.

Speak what we feel, not what we ought to say.

Stars hide your fires; let not light see my black and deep desires: The eyes wink at the hand; yet let that be which the eye fears, when it is done, to see

Summer's lease hath all too short a date.

Suspicion always haunts the guilty mind.

Sweet are the uses of adversity,
Which, like the toad, ugly and venomous,
Wears yet a precious jewel in his head;
And this our life, exempt from public haunt,
Finds tongues in trees, books in the running brooks,
Sermons in stones, and good in every thing.

Sweets to the sweet.

Take it in what sense thou wilt.

Take pains. Be perfect.

Tax not so bad a voice to slander music any more than once.

Tell me where is fancy bred,
Or in the heart, or in the head?

That time of year thou mayst in me behold
When yellow leaves, or none, or few, do hang
Upon those boughs which shake against the cold,
Bare ruin'd choirs, where late the sweet birds sang.
In me thou seest the twilight of such day
As after sunset fadeth in the west,
Which by and by black night doth take away,
Death's second self, that seals up all in rest.
In me thou see'st the glowing of such fire
That on the ashes of his youth doth lie,
As the death-bed whereon it must expire
Consumed with that which it was nourish'd by.
This thou perceivest, which makes thy love more strong,
To love that well which thou must leave ere long.

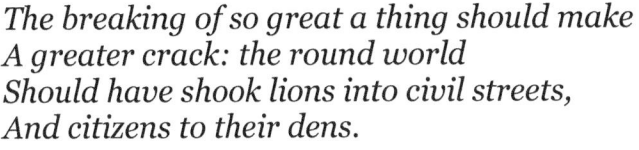

The breaking of so great a thing should make
A greater crack: the round world
Should have shook lions into civil streets,
And citizens to their dens.

The course of true love never did run smooth.

The devil can cite Scripture for his purpose.
An evil soul producing holy witness
Is like a villain with a smiling cheek,
A goodly apple rotten at the heart.
O, what a goodly outside falsehood hath!

The Devil hath power
To assume a pleasing shape.

The evil that men do lives after them;
The good is oft interred with their bones.

The fault, dear Brutus, is not in our stars, but in ourselves.

The first thing we do, let's kill all the lawyers.

The fool doth think he is wise, but the wise man knows himself to be a fool.

The ides of March are come.
Soothsayer: Ay, Caesar; but not gone.

The lady doth protest too much, methinks.

The love that follows us sometime is our trouble, which still we thank as love.

The lunatic, the lover, and the poet, are of imagination all compact.

The man that hath no music in himself, Nor is not moved with concord of sweet sounds, Is fit for treasons, stratagems, and spoils; The motions of his spirit are dull as night, And his affections dark as Erebus. Let no such man be trusted. Mark the music.

The Play's the Thing, wherein I'll catch the conscience of the King.

The prince of darkness is a gentleman!

The quality of mercy is not strained.
It droppeth as the gentle rain from heaven
Upon the place beneath. It is twice blessed:
It blesseth him that gives and him that takes.
'Tis mightiest in the mightiest. It becomes
The thronèd monarch better than his crown.
His scepter shows the force of temporal power,
The attribute to awe and majesty
Wherein doth sit the dread and fear of kings,
But mercy is above this sceptered sway.
It is enthronèd in the hearts of kings.
It is an attribute to God himself.
And earthly power doth then show likest God's
When mercy seasons justice. Therefore, Jew, Though justice
be thy plea, consider this-
That in the course of justice none of us
Should see salvation. We do pray for mercy,
And that same prayer doth teach us all to render
The deeds of mercy. I have spoke thus much
To mitigate the justice of thy plea,
Which if thou follow, this strict court of Venice
Must needs give sentence 'gainst the merchant there.

The rest, is silence.

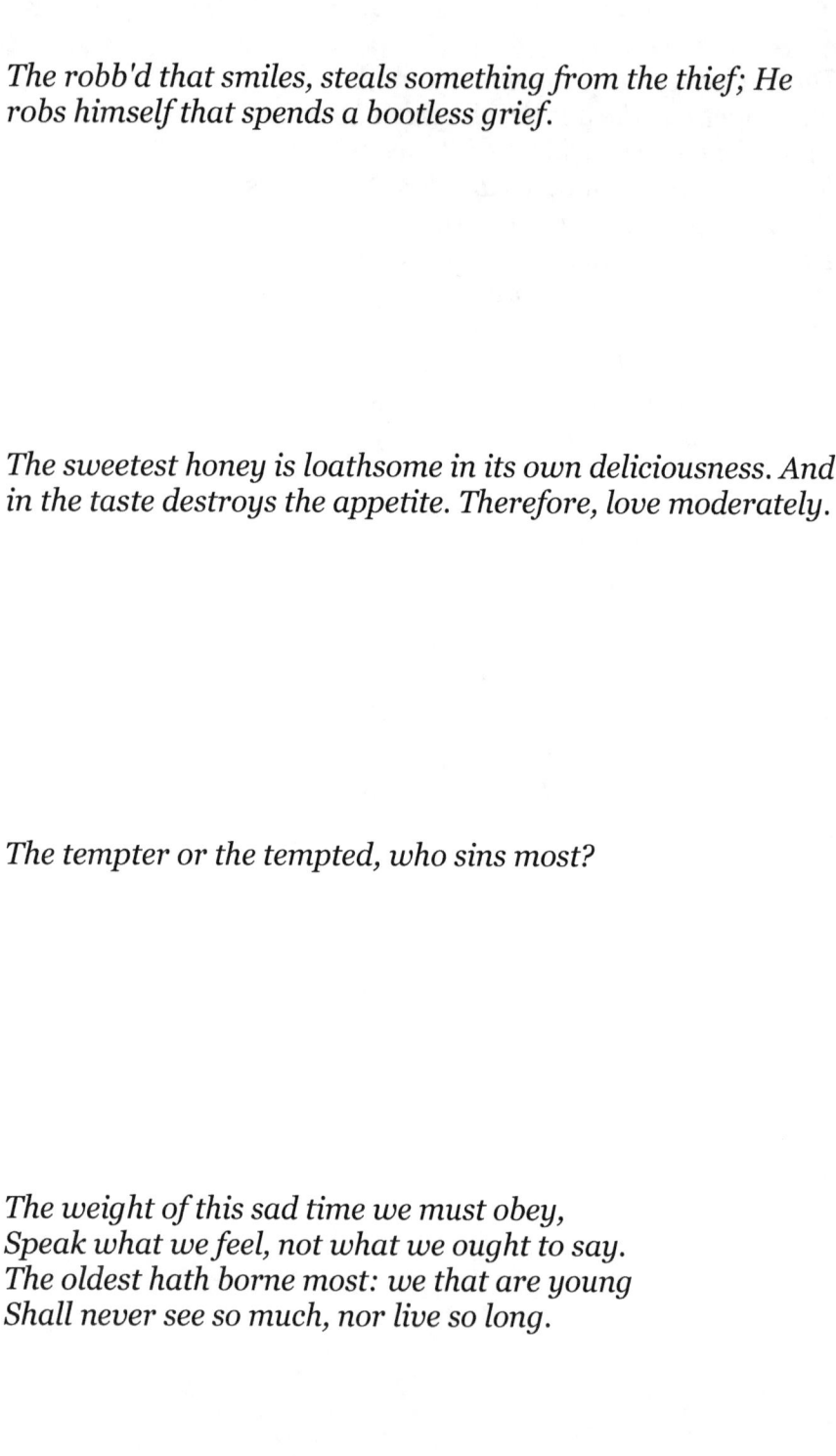

The robb'd that smiles, steals something from the thief; He robs himself that spends a bootless grief.

The sweetest honey is loathsome in its own deliciousness. And in the taste destroys the appetite. Therefore, love moderately.

The tempter or the tempted, who sins most?

*The weight of this sad time we must obey,
Speak what we feel, not what we ought to say.
The oldest hath borne most: we that are young
Shall never see so much, nor live so long.*

Then hate me when thou wilt; if ever, now;
Now, while the world is bent my deeds to cross,
Join with the spite of fortune, make me bow,
And do not drop in for an after-loss:
Ah! do not, when my heart hath 'scaped this sorrow,
Come in the rearward of a conquered woe;
Give not a windy night a rainy morrow,
To linger out a purposed overthrow.
If thou wilt leave me, do not leave me last,
When other petty griefs have done their spite,
But in the onset come: so shall I taste
At first the very worst of fortune's might;
And other strains of woe, which now seem woe,
Compared with loss of thee, will not seem so.

Then is courtesy a turncoat. But it is certain I am loved of all
ladies, only you excepted: and I would I could find in my
heart that I had not a hard heart; for, truly, I love none.

A dear happiness to women: they would else have been
troubled with a pernicious suitor. I thank God and my cold
blood, I am of your humour for that: I had rather hear my
dog bark at a crow than a man swear he loves me. -Much
Ado About Nothing

There are more things in Heaven and Earth, Horatio, than are dreamt of in your philosophy.

There are no tricks in plain and simple faith.

There is a tide in the affairs of men
Which, taken at the flood, leads on to fortune;
Omitted, all the voyage of their life
Is bound in shallows and in miseries.
On such a full sea are we now afloat;
And we must take the current when it serves,
Or lose our ventures.

There is nothing either good or bad, but thinking makes it so.

There is special providence in the fall of a sparrow.

There was a star danced, and under that was I born.

There's a divinity that shapes our ends,
Rough-hew them how we will.

There's an old saying that applies to me: you can't lose a
game if you don't play the game.

There's small choice in rotten apples.

There's rosemary, that's for remembrance; pray, love, remember; and there is pansies, that's for thoughts... There's fennel for you, and columbines; there's rue for you, and here's some for me; we may call it herb of grace o' Sundays. O, you must wear your rue with a difference. There's a daisy. I would give you some violets, but they wither'd all when my father died. They say he made a good end,— [Sings.]
For bonny sweet Robin is all my joy.

These violent delights have violent ends
And in their triumph die, like fire and powder,
Which as they kiss consume. The sweetest honey
Is loathsome in his own deliciousness
And in the taste confounds the appetite.
Therefore love moderately; long love doth so;
Too swift arrives as tardy as too slow.

They do not love that do not show their love.

Thine face is not worth sunburning.

Things base and vile, holding no quantity,
Love can transpose to form and dignity.
Love looks not with the eyes, but with the mind,
And therefore is winged Cupid painted blind.
Nor hath Love's mind of any judgment taste;
Wings and no eyes figure unheedy haste.

Things without all remedy should be without regard: what's
done is done.

This above all: to thine own self be true,
And it must follow, as the night the day,
Thou canst not then be false to any man.

This cold night will turn us all to fools and madmen.

This goodly frame, the earth, seems to me a sterile
promontory, this most excellent canopy, the air, look you, this
brave o'erhanging firmament, this majestical roof fretted
with golden fire, why, it appears no other thing to me than a
foul and pestilent congregation of vapours. What a piece of
work is a man! how noble in reason! how infinite in faculty!
in form and moving how express and admirable! in action
how like an angel! in apprehension how like a god! the
beauty of the world! the paragon of animals! And yet, to me,
what is this quintessence of dust?

This is the excellent foppery of the world, that,
when we are sick in fortune,--often the surfeit
of our own behavior,--we make guilty of our
disasters the sun, the moon, and the stars: as
if we were villains by necessity; fools by
heavenly compulsion; knaves, thieves, and
treachers, by spherical predominance; drunkards,
liars, and adulterers, by an enforced obedience of
planetary influence; and all that we are evil in,
by a divine thrusting on: an admirable evasion
of whoremaster man, to lay his goatish
disposition to the charge of a star.

This royal throne of kings, this sceptered isle, This earth of
majesty, this seat of Mars, This other Eden, demi-paradise,
This fortress built by Nature for herself Against infection and
the hand of war, This happy breed of men, this little world,
This precious stone set in the silver sea, Which serves it in the
office of a wall Or as a moat defensive to a house, Against the
envy of less happier lands,--This blessed plot, this earth, this
realm, this England.

*This thing of darkness I
Acknowledge mine.*

Thou and I are too wise to woo peaceably.

Thou art a very ragged Wart.

Thou mad mustachio purple-hued maltworms!

Thou shouldst not have been old till thou hadst been wise.

Thou weigh'st thy words before thou givest them breath.

Though I am not naturally honest, I am sometimes so by chance.

Though she be but little, she is fierce!

Though this be madness, yet there is method in't.

Thought is free.

Thus I die. Thus, thus, thus.
Now I am dead,
Now I am fled,
My soul is in the sky.
Tongue, lose thy light.
Moon take thy flight.
Now die, die, die, die.

Thus with a kiss I die.

Thy husband is thy lord, thy life, thy keeper,
Thy head, thy sovereign, one that cares for thee,
And for thy maintenance; commits his body
To painful labor, both by sea and land;
To watch the night in storms, the day in cold,
Whilst thou li'st warm at home, secure and safe;
And craves no other tribute at thy hands
But love, fair looks, and true obedience-
Too little payment for so great a debt.
Such duty as the subject owes the prince,
Even such a woman oweth to her husband;
And when she is froward, peevish, sullen, sour,
And no obedient to his honest will,
What is she but a foul contending rebel,
And graceless traitor to her loving lord?
I asham'd that women are so simple
'To offer war where they should kneel for peace,
Or seek for rule, supremacy, and sway,
When they are bound to serve, love, and obey.
Why are our bodies soft, and weak, and smooth,
Unapt to toil and trouble in the world,
But that our soft conditions, and our hearts,
Should well agree with our external parts?

Time travels at different speeds for different people. I can tell
you who time strolls for, who it trots for, who it gallops for,
and who it stops cold for.

Tis an ill cook that cannot lick his own fingers.

Tis in ourselves that we are thus or thus. Our bodies are our gardens to the which our wills are gardeners.

Tis within ourselves that we are thus or thus.

To be honest, as this world goes, is to be one man picked out of ten thousand.

To be, or not to be: that is the question:
Whether 'tis nobler in the mind to suffer
The slings and arrows of outrageous fortune,
Or to take arms against a sea of troubles,
And by opposing end them? To die: to sleep;
No more; and by a sleep to say we end
The heart-ache and the thousand natural shocks
That flesh is heir to, 'tis a consummation
Devoutly to be wish'd. To die, to sleep;
To sleep: perchance to dream: ay, there's the rub;
For in that sleep of death what dreams may come
When we have shuffled off this mortal coil,
Must give us pause: there's the respect
That makes calamity of so long life;
For who would bear the whips and scorns of time,
The oppressor's wrong, the proud man's contumely,
The pangs of despised love, the law's delay,
The insolence of office and the spurns
That patient merit of the unworthy takes,
When he himself might his quietus make
With a bare bodkin? who would fardels bear,
To grunt and sweat under a weary life,
But that the dread of something after death,
The undiscover'd country from whose bourn
No traveller returns, puzzles the will
And makes us rather bear those ills we have
Than fly to others that we know not of?
Thus conscience does make cowards of us all;
And thus the native hue of resolution
Is sicklied o'er with the pale cast of thought,
And enterprises of great pith and moment
With this regard their currents turn awry,
And lose the name of action.--Soft you now!
The fair Ophelia! Nymph, in thy orisons
Be all my sins remember'd!

To-morrow, and to-morrow, and to-morrow,
Creeps in this petty pace from day to day,
To the last syllable of recorded time;
And all our yesterdays have lighted fools
The way to dusty death. Out, out, brief candle!
Life's but a walking shadow, a poor player,
That struts and frets his hour upon the stage,
And then is heard no more. It is a tale
Told by an idiot, full of sound and fury,
Signifying nothing.

True hope is swift, and flies with swallow's wings.

True, I talk of dreams,
Which are the children of an idle brain,
Begot of nothing but vain fantasy,
Which is as thin of substance as the air,
And more inconstant than the wind, who woos
Even now the frozen bosom of the north,
And, being anger'd, puffs away from thence,
Turning his side to the dew-dropping south.

Turn him into stars and form a constellation in his image. His face will make the heavens so beautiful that the world will fall in love with the night and forget about the garish sun.

Two households, both alike in dignity
In fair Verona, where we lay our scene
From ancient grudge break to new mutiny
Where civil blood makes civil hands unclean.
From forth the fatal loins of these two foes
A pair of star-cross'd lovers take their life
Whose misadventured piteous overthrows
Do with their death bury their parents' strife.

Under loves heavy burden do I sink.

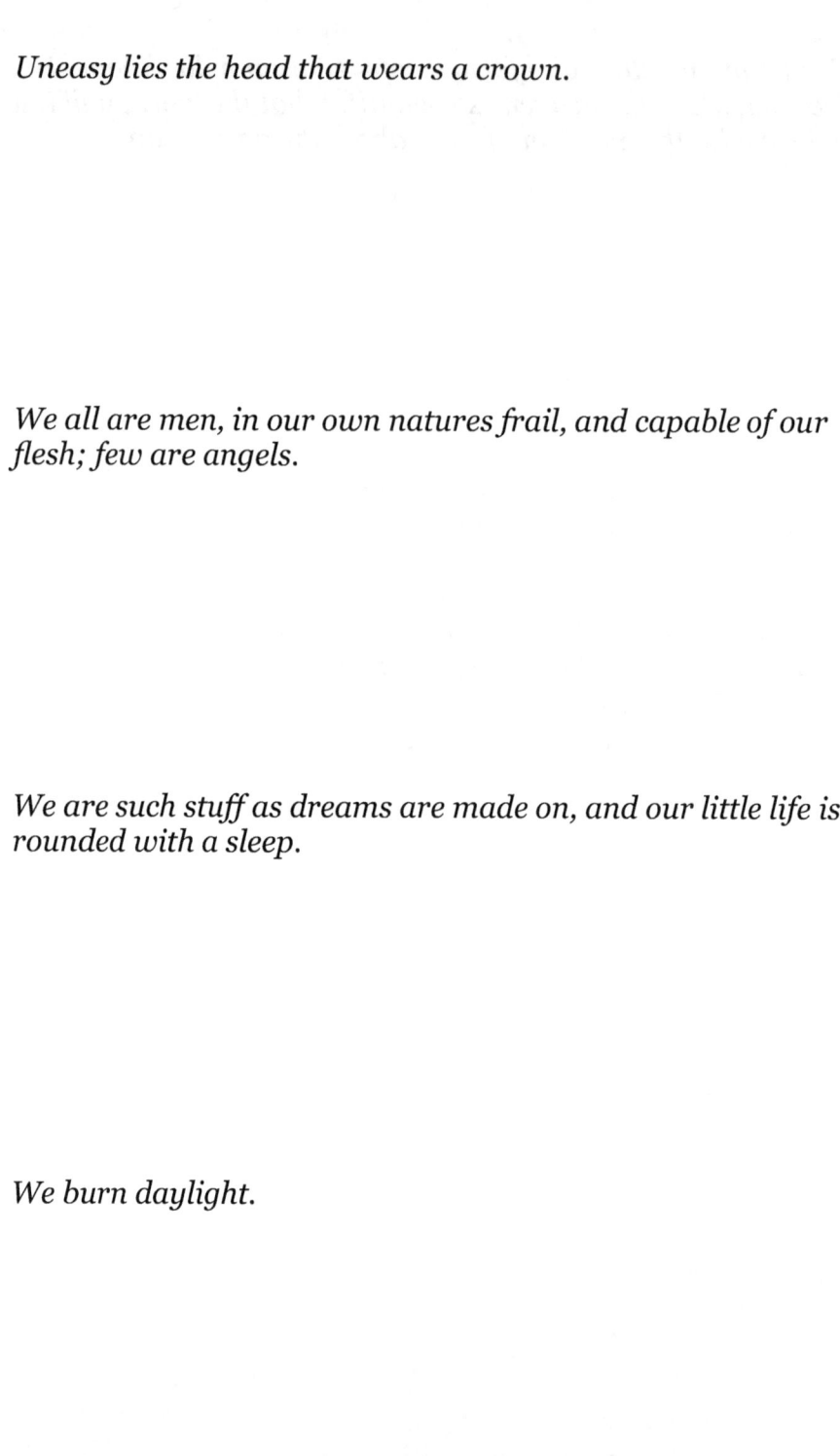

Uneasy lies the head that wears a crown.

We all are men, in our own natures frail, and capable of our flesh; few are angels.

We are such stuff as dreams are made on, and our little life is rounded with a sleep.

We burn daylight.

We know what we are, but not what we may be.

Well, in that hit you miss. She'll not be hit
With Cupid's arrow. She hath Dian's wit,
And, in strong proff of chastity well armed,
From Love's weak childish bow she lives uncharmed.
She will not stay the siege of loving terms,
Nor bide th' encounter of assailing eyes,
Nor ope her lap to saint-seducing gold.
O, she is rich in beauty; only poor
That, when she dies, with dies her store.

WESTMORELAND
O that we now had here
But one ten thousand of those men in England
That do no work to-day!

KING
What's he that wishes so?
My cousin Westmoreland? No, my fair cousin;
If we are mark'd to die, we are enow
To do our country loss; and if to live,
The fewer men, the greater share of honour.

God's will! I pray thee, wish not one man more.
By Jove, I am not covetous for gold,
Nor care I who doth feed upon my cost;
It yearns me not if men my garments wear;
Such outward things dwell not in my desires.
But if it be a sin to covet honour,
I am the most offending soul alive.
No, faith, my coz, wish not a man from England.
God's peace! I would not lose so great an honour
As one man more methinks would share from me
For the best hope I have. O, do not wish one more!
Rather proclaim it, Westmoreland, through my host,
That he which hath no stomach to this fight,
Let him depart; his passport shall be made,
And crowns for convoy put into his purse;
We would not die in that man's company
That fears his fellowship to die with us.
This day is call'd the feast of Crispian.
He that outlives this day, and comes safe home,
Will stand a tip-toe when this day is nam'd,
And rouse him at the name of Crispian.
He that shall live this day, and see old age,
Will yearly on the vigil feast his neighbours,
And say 'To-morrow is Saint Crispian.'
Then will he strip his sleeve and show his scars,
And say 'These wounds I had on Crispian's day.'
Old men forget; yet all shall be forgot,
But he'll remember, with advantages,
What feats he did that day. Then shall our names,
Familiar in his mouth as household words-
Harry the King, Bedford and Exeter,
Warwick and Talbot, Salisbury and Gloucester-
Be in their flowing cups freshly rememb'red.
This story shall the good man teach his son;
And Crispin Crispian shall ne'er go by,
From this day to the ending of the world,
But we in it shall be remembered-
We few, we happy few, we band of brothers;
For he to-day that sheds his blood with me

Shall be my brother; be he ne'er so vile,
This day shall gentle his condition;
And gentlemen in England now-a-bed
Shall think themselves accurs'd they were not here,
And hold their manhoods cheap whiles any speaks
That fought with us upon Saint Crispin's day.

What do I fear? Myself? There's none else by.
Richard loves Richard; that is, I and I.
Is there a murderer here? No. Yes, I am.
Then fly! What, from myself? Great reason why:
Lest I revenge. What, myself upon myself?
Alack, I love myself. Wherefore? For any good
That I myself have done unto myself?
O, no! Alas, I rather hate myself
For hateful deeds committed by myself.
I am a villain. Yet I lie. I am not.
Fool, of thyself speak well. Fool, do not flatter:
My conscience hath a thousand several tongues,
And every tongue brings in a several tale,
And every tale condemns me for a villain.
Perjury, perjury, in the highest degree;
Murder, stern murder, in the direst degree;
All several sins, all used in each degree,
Throng to the bar, crying all, Guilty! guilty!
I shall despair. There is no creature loves me,
And if I die no soul will pity me.
And wherefore should they, since that I myself
Find in myself no pity to myself?

What piece of work is a man, how noble in reason, how infinite in faculties, in form and moving, how express and admirable in action, how like an angel in apprehension, how like a god! The beauty of the world. The paragon of animals. And yet, to me, what is this quintessence of dust?

What win I, if I gain the thing I seek?
A dream, a breath, a froth of fleeting joy.
Who buys a minute's mirth to wail a week?
Or sells eternity to get a toy?
For one sweet grape who will the vine destroy?
Or what fond beggar, but to touch the crown,
Would with the sceptre straight be strucken down?

What, you egg?

What's done cannot be undone.

What's done, is done.

What's in a name? that which we call a rose
By any other name would smell as sweet.

What's past is prologue.

When beggars die, there are no comets seen; the heavens themselves blaze forth the death of princes.

When he shall die,
Take him and cut him out in little stars,
And he will make the face of heaven so fine
That all the world will be in love with night
And pay no worship to the garish sun.

When I bestride him, I soar, I am a hawk: he trots the air; the earth sings when he touches it; the basest horn of his hoof is more musical than the pipe of Hermes.

When I said I would die a bachelor, I did not think I should live till I were married.

When sorrows come, they come not single spies. But in battalions!

When we are born, we cry that we are come to this great stage of fools.

When, in disgrace with fortune and men's eyes,
I all alone beweep my outcast state
And trouble deaf heaven with my bootless cries
And look upon myself and curse my fate,
Wishing me like to one more rich in hope,

Featured like him, like him with friends possess'd,
Desiring this man's art and that man's scope,
With what I most enjoy contented least;
Yet in these thoughts myself almost despising,
Haply I think on thee, and then my state,
Like to the lark at break of day arising
From sullen earth, sings hymns at heaven's gate;
For thy sweet love remember'd such wealth brings
That then I scorn to change my state with kings.

Where shall we three meet again in thunder, lightning, or in
rain? When the hurlyburly 's done, when the battle 's lost and
won

Who could refrain,
That had a heart to love, and in that heart
Courage to make love known?

Who is it that can tell me who I am?

*Who knows himself a braggart, let him fear this, for it will
come to pass that every braggart shall be found an ass.*

*Why then, O brawling love! O loving hate!
O any thing, of nothing first create!
O heavy lightness, serious vanity,
Misshapen chaos of well-seeming forms,
Feather of lead, bright smoke, cold fire, sick health,
Still-waking sleep, that is not what it is!
This love feel I, that feel no love in this.*

*Why, look you now, how unworthy a thing you make of me!
You would play upon me, you would seem to know my stops,*

you would pluck out the heart of my mystery, you would sound me from my lowest note to the top of my compass, and there is much music, excellent voice, in this little organ, yet cannot you make it speak. 'Sblood, do you think I am easier to be played on than a pipe? Call me what instrument you will, though you can fret me, you cannot play upon me.

*Why, man, he doth bestride the narrow world
Like a Colossus; and we petty men
Walk under his huge legs, and peep about
To find ourselves dishonourable graves.*

*Why, what's the matter,
That you have such a February face,
So full of frost, of storm and cloudiness?*

Will all great Neptune's ocean wash this blood clean from my hand? No, this my hand will rather the multitudinous seas incarnadine, making the green one red.

Wisely and slow; they stumble that run fast.

With mirth and laughter let old wrinkles come.

Woe, destruction, ruin, and decay; the worst is death and death will have his day.

Women may fall when there's no strength in men.

Words are easy, like the wind; faithful friends are hard to find.

Words, words, words.

*You are a lover. Borrow Cupid's wings
and soar with them above a common bound.*

You are thought here to the most senseless and fit man for the job.

You cannot, sir, take from me any thing that I will more willingly part withal: except my life, except my life, except my life.

You have witchcraft in your lips, there is more eloquence in a sugar touch of them than in the tongues of the French council; and they should
sooner persuade Harry of England than a general petition of monarchs.

You may my glories and my state depose,
But not my griefs; still am I king of those.

You speak an infinite deal of nothing.

You taught me language, and my profit on't is, I know how to
curse.

Your face, my thane, is as a book where men
May read strange matters. To beguile the time,
Look like the time; bear welcome in your eye,
Your hand, your tongue: look like the innocent flower,
But be the serpent under't.

Your tale, sir, would cure deafness.

www.ingramcontent.com/pod-product-compliance
Lightning Source LLC
Chambersburg PA
CBHW070659100726
47907CB00007B/2273